BOWING

A Moving Meditation for Personal Transformation

BOWING

A Moving Meditation for Personal Transformation

Dahn Yoga Education

BEST Life Media
6560 Highway 179 Ste. 114
Sedona, AZ 86351
www.bestlifemedia.com
1-877-504-1106

First paperback edition: June 2010
Library of Congress Control Number: 2010927128
ISBN: 978-1-935127-44-4

If you are unable to order this book from your local Dahn Yoga or Body + Brain center, you may order through www.bestlifemedia.com.

Mastering others is strength.
Mastering yourself is true power.

—Lao-tzu

Contents

Foreword

Bowing is the most beautiful of human activities.

This statement may seem extreme, but for me it is true. Bowing is an act that represents all of life in its most poetic form. I happen to believe that life is more than just an evolutionary accident. All the struggle, pain, and conflict that we experience happen for a purpose. Bowing is a practice that will impart to you the humility, discipline, and acceptance needed to really see the beauty of this life you lead, and, through its symbolic representation of the greater meaning of life's cyclical process, it will give you the faith and hope you need to keep going forward.

For those who are not familiar with bowing, it may seem strange at first. Often, people associate bowing with worship or some sort of superstition, and so they reject it. They are making a big mistake, I think. Bowing is a natural act, arising in some form in almost every culture around the world, because it is also natural for human beings to seek something bigger than their individual selves.

If you are someone new to bowing, you are very lucky. Yes, there will be sore muscles and perhaps other physical frustrations that accompany any new exercise. But being a beginner is a great gift, for it allows you to approach each bow with a pure, beginner's mind. Use this precious time to establish the proper mind-set and habits to make the most of your bowing practice. It is my sincere wish that this book will be of service to you in that regard.

Bowing is, in essence, about re-creating yourself as you want to be. It is about learning to let go of old things so new things can come to you. During a bowing session, you will raise yourself up, lower yourself down, and then raise yourself up again—over and over until the session is complete. This is like the process of life, a continuous cycle of in and out, up and down. If you want new and better things for your life, you must not resist this cycle. You must be willing to let go of the habits that keep you mired in your current state, as surely as you must exhale before you can inhale.

For most of us in today's culture, it is far easier to take in than to let go. Through years of habit, we have come to value the gathering of things—wealth, possessions, fame, accomplishment. In our frenzy to get more and do more, we have lost sight of the value of emptying ourselves. So much of our lives is centered on earning money, learning new facts, achieving material goals, buying this or that. Living this way is like breathing in and never breathing out. Eventually, our minds become stuffed with information and our environments overflow with material objects. Bowing is a way to get away from all of this busyness for a moment, to finally breathe out. The repetitive, meditative motion offers a simple way to cease the chattering mind so that we may touch on the quiet place that exists inside. By finding and expanding this inner place of stillness, we become vessels for energies much greater than our small selves.

The bow's greatest beauty lies in the symbolic meaning it represents, which is equivalent to the meaning of life itself. In the cyclical up-and-down motion of the bow, we re-create the process through which we accomplish the realization of our highest selves. By bowing over and over again, we bring the reality of this process right into the core of our being, reminding every cell of our bodies that this growth is what life is really all about. The pain and suffering we feel in life can be reduced only by surrendering to the process that the bow represents. Bowing teaches us to surrender to life in a simple, natural way as we tap into our infinite ability to re-create ourselves.

As a practical suggestion, I recommend that you focus on forgiveness as an objective of your bowing practice. Offer forgiveness to all who have harmed you; ask forgiveness for all mistakes you have made; and, most importantly, ask forgiveness from yourself for yourself. Feel gratitude for these things and the growth that they bring.

After you bow, sit quietly and feel your heart. Feel the warmth in your chest as your heart emanates peace and love to the universe. Sit and be still in the moment. In that moment you may realize the illusory nature of all that troubles you.

I hope you find great growth and fulfillment as you embark on this journey. Empty yourself and let the powers of the cosmos fill you up again. This is your birthright and your true source of life.

Ilchi Lee

Introduction

Congratulations. You are about to embark on an amazing journey of personal growth and self-discovery. This is a book about the art of bowing, a practice thousands of years old, yet undiscovered by most people in the West. As you embark on this journey of self-development through bowing, you may view yourself as a kind of pioneer, but what you pioneer has a history as deep and as rich as any of the mind-body practices that you might pursue.

While you may not be familiar with the use of bowing as a discipline, in reality it is a universal activity. Most cultures around the world use bowing in some form or another. All of the world's major religions use some form of bowing, during prayer or other devotional activities. As an everyday part of life, it is especially associated with Eastern cultures, where people commonly bow to each other as a mutual sign of respect. Even in the West, people bow when receiving applause at the end of a performance. And only a few hundred years ago, people in Europe regularly bowed to royalty and other superiors to show submission to these authority figures.

Bowing as a mind-body development technique is something a little different. In this case, you are not bowing to some person or god. It is similar to other types of bowing in the sense that it incorporates the element of humility, but it is not about showing your humility or deference to some other human being. And it is definitely not about worshipping someone or something.

Rather, bowing as we speak of it is about cultivation of self. When you bow, you are doing it for only one person—*you*. You bow to make your mind calmer, your body fitter, your whole being focused toward creating a better life for yourself.

The kind of bowing introduced to you in this book reflects the meeting of East and West that permeates today's interconnected world. It has sometimes been suggested that the East is becoming westernized, and the West is becoming easternized. In the Asian countries, this process is perhaps more obvious, as industrialization rapidly develops and Western cultural elements take root. In the West, however, the transformation is less obvious, and it involves going inward and becoming more still, rather than more active. The bowing process includes a balance of active and contemplative elements—of the *yin* and the *yang*, to put it in Taoist terminology—but it is the going inward that is of greatest value to most practitioners.

Keep in mind that bowing can be whatever you choose to make it. It can potentially benefit all three aspects of the human being: body, mind, and spirit. A key principle of energy training is "energy goes where the mind goes." The same is true here. If you focus on achieving physical benefits, that is likely the result you will get. If you focus on more spiritual concerns, you will see change in that area. The important thing is to focus on *something*. Have a clear goal in mind, and use bowing to open yourself to success in that area.

Whatever goal you have in mind as you begin bowing training, the most important attribute is sincerity. It is useless to begin training without a deep commitment to your own self-development. In fact, bowing practice is sometimes referred to as "sincerity training." Through bowing, you will develop the serious, focused attitude you need to create whatever it is you want for yourself, and you will shed any negativity or lack of commitment that may be holding you back. In this way, bowing becomes much more than a simple, repetitive exercise as it cultivates the focus and determination you will need to transform your life.

The postures you take during bowing symbolize this process of transformation. As you will learn in detail in chapter 5(page 57), each phase of the bow has specific meaning. The bow begins with upward motion of the arms, then the body is lowered to the ground, and then you rise again. This movement refers not only to the overall life and death process but also to the many cycles of rising and falling, and expanding and contracting, that compose the various phases of life.

Ultimately, bowing is about developing internal and external grace. It exists only for your own self-reflection and self-reverence. However you choose to practice it, whether occasionally or consistently, always remember that each bow is nothing but a conversation with your own true nature. You are the sacred element within the bow; you will not find it in the physical form of the bow, in your instructor's recommendations, or in a particular number of bows that you perform. By keeping your True Self, above all other things, at the center of your bowing practice, you will undoubtedly develop a deep, abiding acceptance of yourself and your humble, yet magnificent place within the universe.

Chapter 1

Bowing as a Mind-Body Practice

Sometimes people are a little surprised when they are first introduced to bowing as a self-development method. People in Western cultures are accustomed to thinking of bowing in terms of worship or subservience, so it may seem odd to them at first. Practices like yoga and meditation also seemed strange when they were first introduced to popular culture in the 1960s and 1970s, but over time they have become well accepted. Bowing, however, has not yet been as widely assimilated, perhaps because of the preexisting associations people have connected to the physical act of bowing. Once they get past these associations, however, most people find the practice highly rewarding and personally transformative.

In reality, bowing has existed in some form in virtually every culture on Earth. Since Charles Darwin published his landmark book *The Expression of the Emotions in Man and Animals*, people have realized that certain facial gestures and expressive movements are universal in meaning and form. Bowing, just like smiling and frowning, is one of these universal gestures. In fact, even nonhuman social animals, like wolves and chimpanzees, make similar sorts of gestures to indicate a lower position in rank and the desire to concede to superiors. So the predecessor to bowing can be seen in the universal tendency to lower one's head, or even cower, when in the presence of authority figures.

Of course human forms of bowing have progressed along with civilization and are far more sophisticated than the gestures of animals. Bowing is not necessarily about showing submission to rank or authority but about internal grace and humility from within the self. Sometimes, bowing is quite elaborate and elegant, such as its use in Asian tea ceremonies. In this case, the objective is the brewing of fine tea, but bowing and other ceremonial features add to the highly formalized, symbolic nature of the event.

The practice and meaning of bowing in human culture can vary dramatically depending on context. Sometimes, it is indeed similar to the instinctual reactions of animals, as when a subject genuflects to a king, showing submission in a way that is not dissimilar to animals' displays of subjugation. But there are many more subtle forms of bowing in both Eastern and Western cultures. Because Western cultures have deliberately moved away from rigid hierarchies toward democratic models, bowing has been largely discarded as inegalitarian and undemocratic.

Eastern cultures have also moved away from old feudal systems, yet bowing persists as an integral, evolving part of culture. When people greet each other in places like Japan, China, and Korea, the greeting will often include a modest bow to indicate basic respect for the other person. If the person you greet is of much higher rank, you might be expected to bow deeply to indicate your recognition of that person. By the same token, if the person you meet is a child or much lower in rank in comparison with you, you may not be expected to bow at all. Sometimes, bowing will involve bringing the entire body to the ground, as in the Chinese *kowtow*, which requires the individual, often someone who has been shamed for some reason, to bring the forehead all the way to the ground in front of the seated, superior individual. In Korea, individuals used to perform one full-body bow to show appreciation for parents and three bows to show deference to enlightened spiritual masters.

In Western cultures, bowing has evolved differently. At one time, the practice of "bowing and scraping" to one's superiors was a common part of feudal European culture. Today, the growing emphasis on personal civil rights and individual empowerment has caused bowing to become less common than it once was, although a quick nod of the head when greeting someone is not an uncommon sight in most Western cultures. That being said, bowing continues to exist in many noticeable forms in the West. For example, people in Europe will still gladly bow or curtsy to the king or queen of their country, even though the role of these non-elected monarchs as rulers is often largely symbolic. People today also bow or curtsy when receiving applause after a performance, as a way to show humility in the face of adulation.

Both East and West have in common the use of bowing in a religious context. All the major religions—Christianity, Judaism, Islam, and Buddhism—use bowing in some form or another. Perhaps it could be said that while people's conception of human authority systems change, humanity's subservience to god and spiritual principles always remains. These religious manifestations of bowing may range from a simple bowing of the head in prayer to kneeling before an altar to a full prostration of the body on the ground. The Eastern Orthodox Catholic Church includes an elaborate system of bowing monitored by strict rules about the degree and depth of the bow. In some cases, individuals place their entire body flat on the ground to show humility before God. Similarly, monks from certain branches of Buddhism go on long pilgrimages during which they prostrate their bodies along the entire way, traveling only one body length at a time.

The one underlying element that all forms of bowing have in common is their connection to the human attribute of humility. This does not, however, necessarily mean humility toward another person, or even to a god. But it does mean humility in the sense of acceptance and acknowledgement one's ultimate dependence on the gifts of life and consciousness that are given to you. And it also means accepting yourself as you are now, so that you will be able to accept fully the person you are meant to become.

The bowing practice described here has evolved from these spiritual forms of bowing, but it is not necessarily performed for spiritual reasons. A similar form of bowing is used quite commonly in Buddhist practice, and it is practiced for both religious and secular reasons. Primarily, the bowing practice that we are advocating here is purely for your personal self-development and should not be considered part of any one particular religion. As you will discover, bowing is worth doing simply because it is good for you—physically, mentally, and spiritually.

Today, there is a lot of competition for your physical fitness time and money. You have only to turn on the radio or TV for a few minutes until you see some advertisement for the latest, greatest fitness trend. A lot of money is spent to get you to try the latest diet, to buy health experts' books, and to use some ingenious gadget that promises health and fitness. But, if you've tried any of these things, you know how often they leave people feeling disappointed. Most people spend money on these things, try them for a couple of weeks, and return to their habits. The novelty and effectiveness of these products usually disappear quickly.

The greatest thing about bowing is that it is completely cost-free and is one of the most convenient and practical exercise forms that you could possibly imagine. Bowing requires no special equipment and can be practiced anywhere and at any time. Even when you are traveling, you can easily bow in the privacy of your hotel room.

In essence, mind-body training is about developing the attribute of discipline. For many people, developing self-discipline is difficult because of busy schedules and cluttered lives. Yoga, tai chi, and the like are effective, but it can be difficult to find time to go to the gym, studio, or park to receive special instruction. Inevitably, people start out with great intentions, only to fizzle out within a month or so. With bowing, the location is wherever you are, and no special instruction is required.

There has not yet been much scientific investigation of bowing and its effects, but anecdotal evidence is strong. In South Korea, where bowing is a much more common practice, a television documentary investigated its effectiveness. It showed how for many people it has evolved into something more than a religious practice and has now been adopted as a simple health routine. As part of the investigation, the reporters had a group of people with diabetes try bowing as exercise, and another group walking, for four weeks. The bowing group showed greater improvement in muscle mass, stress reduction, and blood sugar levels.

The best thing is to simply give it a try and see how it feels to you. It is entirely an experiential type of training, and it is only through actual practice that you can judge its suitability for you. A lot of people, even if resistant at first, find it very natural once they try it. Here is one practitioner's recollection of starting to bow:

The very first time I experienced bowing I felt like I had found an old friend. My body felt like waves in an ocean, rising and falling to rhythm, connecting heaven and Earth through my body. Every day it is still the same comforting, cleansing, joyful experience. I don't think I will ever tire of it. (Kathy Hallock, Honolulu, HI)

As a mind-body practice, bowing is similar to meditation, but it is a moving meditation. Repetition, such as the use of chanting and prayer beads, is a common tool to help people achieve a meditative state. The Buddhist writer Thich Nhat Hanh, in his famous essay "Driving Meditation," explains how driving, or any other prolonged activity, can become a kind of meditation, so long as one's mind-set is right. This is even truer for bowing, since it is designed to help quiet your thinking mind, the ultimate goal of all meditation practice. Bowing does not have any specific outcome attached to it and with practice can become practically automatic. Many people find it far easier to follow a moving meditation of this sort than to sit for long hours in the half-lotus posture.

As you begin your bowing practice, you may find that it is a bit awkward or physically difficult. One six-year practitioner describes her initial experience like this:

I had a very big problem with my knees, so the first time I only finished three bows. I had to use my hands to boost myself up and down. After one month of daily practice, I was finally able to do one hundred bows. My knees had recovered 100 percent. My legs got into very good shape, I increased my stamina, my mind has become clearer. I have also become more creative and peaceful, and very successful in my life. (Yelena Krasnov, San Ramon, CA)

If you are not in the best physical shape or feel a bit intimidated by bowing, don't worry. You are doing this only for yourself, and you need do only what is comfortable and appropriate for you. Over time, you will find that your practice naturally evolves into what you need it to be.

Chapter 2

Bowing for All Levels of Self

*I*f you would like to transform yourself, you know that you must go far beyond the surface level. True health is not just the absence of disease in the body but a radiant sense of wellness that permeates your entire being. One of the greatest things about bowing is the fact that it is a single exercise that provides benefit in all three realms of wellness, including body, mind, and spirit.

If you were to spend only fifteen minutes a day on an exercise regimen, bowing might be your best option. The most obvious physical benefit is to the musculoskeletal system. With each bow, you engage all muscle groups of the body at some point, both stretching and contracting them. When you first begin, you may feel some soreness in your muscles, but don't worry—that is just evidence that your muscles are being worked and developed. Through bowing, you can maintain all of your muscles at a basic level of fitness, avoiding the atrophy that comes through disuse and a sedentary lifestyle.

One of the most important sets of muscles are your leg muscles. Studies have shown that leg strength is one of the most accurate indicators of longevity because legs allow us to maintain mobility and an active way of life. Unfortunately, many of us sit far too much during the day, leading to poor leg muscle development and lack of stamina. As you bow, you will undoubtedly notice that the legs are being worked considerably, which helps counteract the effects of a sedentary lifestyle.

All of the joints of your body are also used during bowing. The knees, shoulder joints, spine, and hip joints are fully used, which helps keep these typical problem areas from becoming problems later on in life. In addition, joints that you may rarely consider are stretched and opened, such as the toe joints and wrists.

If you experience stiffness or pain in any of your joints, you will likely find that bowing helps loosen and smooth the joint's function, thereby increasing range of motion in that joint. Bowing also moves the joints in novel ways, thus reducing the negative impact of daily, repetitive use. But be sure to exercise caution and modify your bow if needed, especially in the case of serious back or knee issues.

Many types of exercise can lead to injury because they do not use the body in a balanced symmetrical way (Sisson). Most sports require the use of one side of the body more than the other, which leads to problems like tennis elbow. Sometimes even daily, imbalanced use of the body leads to these problems, as in the case of carpal tunnel syndrome. Other exercises are symmetrical, but cause disproportionate impact on one area of the body, such as the knee joints during running. Bowing is not likely to lead to any of these problems because it is both balanced and low impact, helping create a strong, well-aligned body.

Bowing will also improve circulation throughout the body. Most obviously, because it is a light form of aerobic exercise, it will help circulate blood through the cardiovascular system. The expanding and contracting motions of bowing will also help move lymph through the lymph system, which is dependent on the body's movement to keep circulating (Bresloff). One practitioner reports that she loves to start her day with morning bows. She says, "My whole body gets a nice stretch, and I feel like all my blood starts flowing. It feels so comfortable and cozy. A great start to the morning" (Stephanie Jasieniecki, Bloomfield, NJ).

You might think, if you are short on time, that you would be better off doing something more intense, such as running. However, health experts are now recommending less strenuous workouts, such as walking, for general fitness for most people. This is because studies have shown that intense exercise routines are hard to maintain and may cause more harm than good by creating wear and tear on the body. Also, if you desire to lose weight, a lighter workout will burn fat more readily than a strenuous one.

Most people report feeling a significant reduction in stress and tension when they bow regularly. Its repetitive motion is calming, producing results similar to any rocking motion, such as that in a rocking chair or hammock. Furthermore, it stretches the muscles and encourages deep, full breaths, both of which help release tension from the body. Since stress has been clearly linked to the development of disease, this is a significant benefit (Wein).

But did you know that bowing is also a form of energy training? Just like yoga, ki gong, and tai chi, it can help you feel and move energy throughout your body. Yet, compared with those other practices, it is easy to learn, involving just one continuous movement, rather than dozens of different postures. If practiced regularly, bowing can help you maintain your sense of vitality and help increase your awareness of how energy works in your body.

While the concept of energy still has not gained complete acceptance from Western allopathic doctors, in Asian medicine it forms the foundation of the way doctors look at their patients and evaluate their complaints. For them, disease is the result not of some outside influence but of some energy imbalance or blockage. Acupuncturists and herbalists work less to eradicate the disease than to return the body to a state of balance and proper energy flow.

In the East, this energy is known as *ki* (or *chi* or *qi*). The systems of medicine that are founded on this belief are based in thousands of years of observation, although it is hard to document scientifically because it is invisible. Ki energy is thought to run through the body via a series of channels called meridians. By opening up these channels, you will be able to facilitate healing and to develop a deep sense of well-being. The various stages of the bow help open various groups of meridians through the natural movement of the bow.

- Bringing your palms together over your head at the beginning of the bow opens the meridians in the arms and chest.
- Bending forward stimulates the center line of the body, the conception meridian, as well as the meridians running along the back of the legs.
- Lowering your body to the ground stimulates the meridians on the front of the legs and feet.

In addition to the meridians, there are a series of energy centers called chakras. The seven main chakras run along the center line of the body, from the top of the head to the perineum. Each chakra represents some aspect of the human being. If you struggle in some area of your life, you may have some blockage in the corresponding chakra. The up-and-down, expanding and contracting motion of the bow cleans and stimulates these chakras.

In Dahn Yoga we emphasize three of these chakras, which we call *dahn-jons*. The lower dahn-jon is equivalent to the second chakra (also known as the sacral chakra) and is the powerhouse of the body, providing physical strength and vitality. The middle dahn-jon, which corresponds to the fourth chakra (also known as the heart chakra), is the

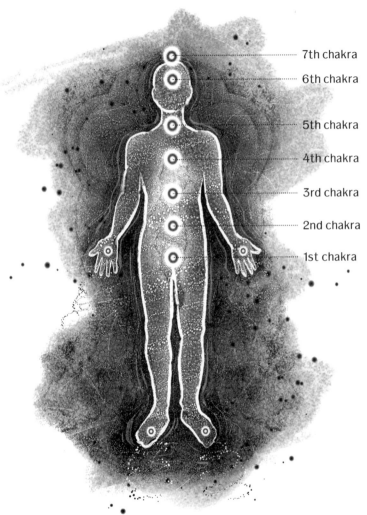

7th chakra

6th chakra

5th chakra

4th chakra

3rd chakra

2nd chakra

1st chakra

(Chakra System)

source of our mental and emotional energies. The upper dahn-jon, identical to the sixth chakra (also known as the "third eye"), is associated with spiritual experience and insight.

There are also four secondary energy centers known as "external dahn-jons." Two are located on the palms (called *jang-shim* points), and two are located on the bottoms of the feet (called *yong-chun* points). These four points are important because they are where all the meridian lines come together. Stimulating these points is like stimulating the entire meridian system at once.

- When you bring your forehead to the ground near the end of the bow, it helps stimulate the upper dahn-jon and your spiritual insight.
- The bending and straightening of the spine helps clear the middle dahn-jon, leading to a calmer mind and more settled emotions.
- The lower dahn-jon is strengthened by lifting the body off the ground and breathing to the lower abdomen.
- Bringing the palms together makes a complete circuit of the meridian system. When you bring your jang-shim to the

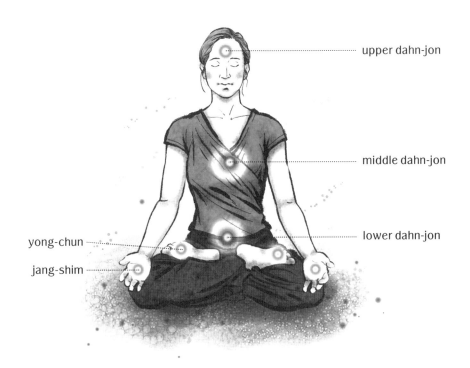

upper dahn-jon

middle dahn-jon

lower dahn-jon

yong-chun

jang-shim

(Dahn-jon System)

ground you connect to the Earth. When you turn them over, you receive heavenly energy.

❧ When you lower your body to the ground and lift it up again, the yong-chun points are stimulated and opened.

Bowing also helps create and maintain proper balance of hot and cold energies in your body. The ideal balance is called *su seung hwa gang*, which translates literally as "water up, fire down." When we are healthy and peaceful, cool water energy rises upward, keeping our head cool and calm, and hot fire energy gathers in the lower abdomen. When we are sick or upset, the flow reverses itself, causing hot energy to gather in the head and the abdomen to become cold. If you have ever been extremely angry or had a fever, you have probably noticed this effect. Many people today have reversed energy flow because of stress or emotional blockages.

Bowing helps reestablish proper flow of energy through its up-and-down, expanding and contracting pumping action, which encourages water energy to rise from the kidneys up to the head, while the strenuous leg activity builds heat in the lower abdomen. This effect has been confirmed by one study created for a Korean television documentary.

Dr. Byungsoo Ku, an Eastern medicine practitioner from Dongook University in South Korea, compared people who walked for ten minutes with those who bowed 108 times. The bowing group maintained a higher lower-body temperature and a lower upper-body temperature than the walking group.

Some practitioners report that bowing feels similar to ki gong, a form of free-flowing energy training. Once the postures become familiar to you, you may begin to feel this. The movement will seem to flow naturally and effortlessly, like waves rolling one after another onto a beach. Allow your breath to naturally coordinate with the movements, breathing in as you draw your arms overhead, breathing out as you lower yourself to the floor. Feel the energy expand and contract throughout your body as you follow the motion. One advanced practitioner describes the feeling this way:

Energetically, I feel my body expanding without borders. It feels like there is no separation between my body and the space around me. It feels like my being is filling the whole space. I feel many paradoxical or opposite states exist simultaneously. Emptiness and fulfillment, expansion and contraction, a moment spreading to the eternal, time

*stops but space flows, being humble and being magnificent, stillness
and a subtle, rhythmic vibration . . . (Ji Young Oh, Sedona, AZ)*

As you begin to sense energy more clearly through your bowing practice, you will have found a great key to personal healing and transformation. Physicists, in studying the atom's structure, have shown that everything is really just energy. As you begin to sense energy directly, you will begin to understand that you are not limited by the apparent limitations of the body. You will start to balance your energies to work with the flow of life itself.

Chapter 3

Bowing and Your Brain

*I*n his Brain Education philosophies, Ilchi Lee boils down the human value system to three simple needs: health, happiness, and peace. He emphasizes bowing because it helps create these three things within the human being. We have seen the health benefits, but what about happiness and peace? Lee teaches that these two things can happen only in the brain, and so he emphasizes the brain as the key to creating happiness and peace, on both the personal and the global levels. After all, it is through your brain that you make all your decisions and feel all your emotions. If you begin to consider how your brain functions in day-to-day life, you will see that you must change your brain to change your life in any meaningful way.

But how do we create happiness and peace in the brain? And how could something like bowing help in that process? In fact, a sense of joy and peace are the most common benefits reported by practitioners. One describes it this way:

When I bow, I usually feel incredibly happy and grateful. Sometimes it is almost overwhelming; I can't stop smiling or laughing. It is hard to explain where it comes from, but I feel that it is because bowing is a time that I get to connect to myself, and this is how my body shows me that it likes that very much. (Nathan Guadagni, West Linn, OR)

Like any exercise, bowing promotes an overall sense of well-being. Studies have shown that exercise releases hormones like serotonin and endorphins that help generate feelings of relaxation and contentment (Ernst). Some people report that by beginning their day with a session of bowing, they are able to maintain a sense of peace and tranquillity all day, even when conditions are difficult.

Bowing goes beyond ordinary exercise, however, because it helps practitioners gain greater control over the workings of the mind. One person describes her early experiences with bowing:

When I first started to bow, I was in an emotionally crazy place. My instructor showed me how to bow and told me to listen to my true self. I had an amazing experience because I heard the truth and was in the greatest peace I'd known in a really long time. (Christie Jensen, West Linn, OR)

The mental benefits of bowing are more dramatic than regular exercises because bowing is a form of meditation and can serve a similar purpose. Like any other form of meditation, bowing helps clean the clutter of the mind. This is not an easy task because the mind normally races with an endless procession of ideas and information, especially in today's fast-paced, computerized world. Bowing occupies the mind with a simple, repetitive set of movements, which distracts the mind from the chaos of thoughts. In a way, bowing allows you to get to know yourse' again, especially when you have been distracted by excess informa' or bothersome emotions.

As you have seen, the bow represents humility in a profound sense; the ability to control one's emotions comes through the ability to control one's ego. Emotions, after all, come from the ego, which is primarily concerned with fulfilling its own individual desires. When the ego's wants, needs, or expectations are not met, negative emotions result; when the ego's desires are fulfilled, the ego is happy and content.

The ego is not bad per se, but it is a part of us that must be placed in check for the sake of our inner and outer happiness. If the ego is allowed to rule the show, we are also ruled by our emotions. It is only through a certain level of humility that we are able to let go of negative emotions, and heal ourselves and our relationships.

If you would like to clear away old, hurtful emotions through bowing, focus on three important values.

- ❧ **Gratitude:** This trait can help us realize the value in even the most difficult circumstances. Focusing on all the many blessings in your life will make the difficult things seem small and insignificant.
- ❧ **Open heartedness:** During training, focus on opening your heart to everything and everyone, even the people and situa-

tions that have hurt you. As you bow, try to literally feel your heart chakra becoming warmer as it begins to vibrate with joy.

🌿 **Responsibility:** Part of having a humble mind means acknowledging your role in any situation. Remember that you are primarily responsible for your own growth, not that of others. No matter how much you may feel someone else is to blame for something in your life, you can change the situation only by changing yourself.

Bowing may not seem like brain training to you, but really it is. It is a common part of Ilchi Lee's Brain Education method, embraced by thousands of practitioners around the world. Bowing provides a good foundation for practice because it incorporates the first three steps of the training process and continues as a unifying element in the final two.

The first step of Brain Education is called Brain Sensitizing. During this stage, practitioners become aware of their brain in relation to their health and well-being. Many of the exercises at this point are simple mind-body exercises designed to improve connection between the brain and body. Bowing is part of this process, helping practitioners evaluate and improve brain abilities like balance and coordination.

Brain Versatilizing is the second step of Brain Education. The exercises used during this phase help the brain become more flexible, able to adapt to new situations and learn new things. This part of the practice draws on the brain's ability to change itself, something called neuroplasticity. Bowing, like any exercise, increases the number of connections between neurons as the practitioner moves his or her body in novel ways (Aamodt). Although bowing may seem awkward at first, this is actually great for the brain because every time you try something new, you create new pathways in the brain. These pathways will help you learn and remember things more easily in the future.

The next step in the method is referred to as Brain Refreshing. At this point participants try to let go of old, damaging thought patterns and emotions. Bowing is highly effective for calming and cleansing the mind, and it is often used by practitioners for precisely this end. Through this "cleansing" effect, bowing helps people re-create themselves by getting rid of burdensome information. In this sense, bowing can also help facilitate the ability to focus and learn new things, since emotions can often block these brain abilities.

The final two steps are Brain Integrating and Brain Mastering, both of which help practitioners use the brain well in all aspects of their lives. Most advanced Brain Education practitioners continue to bow as a foundational part of their practice because it reinforces the achievements gained in the earlier steps. It becomes part of the process by which they gain control over the information in the brain, and it provides a tool for clearing the mind of anything that may be blocking the achievement of personal goals.

Bowing is also a wonderful opportunity to change negative habits. First of all, negative habits often have an emotional root, so by cleansing and clearing old emotions, you have already made great strides toward change (Young). Experts also say that the best way to get rid of a habit is to replace it with another, more positive one. If you are able to maintain your commitment to bowing, you will have created a positive habit for yourself that you can be proud of.

You may wish to use bowing as a way to focus on some goal you have set for yourself. Bowing can work well in this way because it can leave the practitioner calm and open to new ways of thinking. If you set your intentions clearly, you might be surprised at what you can accomplish.

If you wish to gain significant benefit through bowing, watch your mind closely as you bow. It is critical to be sincere about your practice. To gain benefit, you must be there for yourself alone, not to impress anyone else. Remember that bowing is not a sport, and there is little use in comparing your progress with others. It only pays to measure yourself against yourself, for that is the only measurement of growth that will lead to more growth.

Chapter 4

Bowing for Spiritual Growth

All of life is about growth. If you look around, you will see that this is what every living thing is struggling to do. Whether plant or animal, everything is pushing forward, trying to live better than the day before. Your life, with all of its trials and tribulations, is just another representation of this life force.

This is not only true on the physical plane; it is true for the soul as well. In fact, you could say that the physical plane merely exists to help the soul grow. If we focus on the soul's growth, all the struggles of life have meaning and utility.

The humbling process of bowing is also a representation of the soul's growth process. By humbling ourselves, we actually lift our real self up as our small self is subdued. Symbolically in the bow, we slay our small self, which in turn gives rise to the growth of the True Self. Shunryu uzuki, a Zen master and the author of *Zen Mind, Beginner's Mind*, describes it this way:

> *By bowing, we are giving up ourselves to the universe. To give up ourselves means to give up our dualistic ideas and become one. When you become one with everything that exists, you find the true meaning of being.*

An ancient 5,000-year-old Korean document called the *Chun Bu Kyung* attempts to explain the meaning of life and our place in the universe. It consists of eighty-one script characters that speak of the design of the universe and humanity's function within it. According to this document, human beings are meant to serve as a bridge between heaven and Earth, uniting both the physical and the divine. The meaning is difficult to understand directly, but even just hearing the sound of the words can communicate a lot. Many practitioners like to memorize it

天符經

一始無始一析三極無
盡本天一一地一二人
一三一積十鉅無匱化
三天二三地二三人二
三大三合六生七八九
運三四成環五七一妙
衍萬往萬來用變不動
本本心本太陽昂明人
中天地一一終無終一

(Chun Bu Kyung)

and chant it during bowing. It can be hard to memorize, so another option is to play an audio recording of others chanting it, such as on the audio recording *The Power of the Chun Bu Kyung* (available at www. bestlifemedia.com).

In Dahn Yoga practice it is common, but not necessary, to bring the *Chun Bu Kyung* into the bowing process, since it explains the same truth that the bow represents.

In the bowing process, you will see a representation of these two elements, heaven and Earth, coming together through the human body. When you raise your hands up at the beginning of the bow, it represents your spirit rising toward heaven. Then you carry heaven's energy down into the human form as you draw your hands down, which represents your soul coming into this human life.

When you kneel to the ground in humility, it represents connecting to the Earth, the mother of all life. Interestingly, the English word *humble* comes from the Latin word *humus*, which means "earth" or "ground." By acknowledging our total dependence on the Earth, we step for a moment beyond the confines of our egos. When we place the third eye on the ground, it represents a meeting between the divine and the earthly realms. In a handbook for Catholic Benedictine monks, who commonly prostrate themselves on the ground in prayer, the act of bowing is described in this way:

The bow is an expression of gratitude for the utter giftedness of life itself in this very moment. We bow to the ground, the Earth, Mother Earth, of which we are a part, but in doing so we are also bowing to the "ground" of all that is, God, Source, and Sustainer of all that is . . . thus the bow is a gesture of communion with all that lives within the mercy of God . . . we bow in acknowledgement of this central, ongoing mystery. In some mysterious way, the bow contains our whole life. . . . Even if you can't do anything but bow, if done as an expression of who you really are, it contains everything.

But bowing does not end with one humbled and on the ground forever. Rather, this act of humility leads immediately to a rising once again to the heavens, for it is through this act of lowering the small self that the soul comes closer to being reunited once again with heaven.

The act of bowing is a practice designed to help you recognize the ultimate Oneness of all things in the universe. It helps us overcome the ego, which continuously feeds us delusions of separation from the whole.

By repeating the movement, we can come to a deep, cell-level understanding and acceptance of our real place and purpose in the world.

Many people seek a kind of rebirth through spiritual practice. The bow represents both the withering away of the old self and the regeneration of a purer, truer self. One Dahn master puts it this way:

When I do bows, I experience my body, mind, and energy become reborn naturally. When I do bows, I cast my desires, attachments, emotions, and all other distractions into the void. When I empty myself fully, the energy of the universe enters my body and my purer energies emerge. When I am in a purer state, I can see clearly what I really want, and I realize that I already have the power I need within me. (Chunsuk Lee, Cottonwood, AZ)

To overcome the obstacles of life is to overcome the ego and to grow the soul, and so it is wise to set deliberate goals for one's growth. You can do this through bowing, too, by setting simple goals for your bowing practice. You might, for example, decide to do a certain number of bows for a certain number of days. You do not have to be hard on yourself if you fail in this kind of goal, just use it as a way to watch your habits and your internal dialogue.

You are free to do any number of bows, but sometimes people choose the number based on its symbolic value. You can also just set a length of time to bow, such as fifteen minutes, thirty minutes, or an hour. Please start with no more than twenty-one bows and work up to a larger number as you progress. Here is what the numbers typically represent:

- ❧ 3—ultimate unity of heaven/Earth/human and body/mind/ spirit
- ❧ 9—the above trinity through three sets of three
- ❧ 21—renewal and rebirth, since it takes twenty-one days for a bird's egg to hatch
- ❧ 49—based on the seven chakras, this number represents seven times seven
- ❧ 103—the number one hundred represents completion because ten is the number of perfection, and ten times ten equals one hundred; three bows are added to represent heaven, Earth, and human
- ❧ 360—the completion of a cycle, since there are 360 degrees in a circle

❧ **1,000**—for experienced practitioners, one thousand represents deep purification because ten is the number of perfection; if you complete one thousand bows, you have done ten sets of one hundred bows

As you read the next chapter, you will find that the process of the bow is equated with the cycle of life, as represented in the blooming and wilting of a flower. As you progress on your journey, try to keep this image of the blossoming flower in the back of your mind, and soon you, too, will bloom into a vibrant new being.

Chapter 5

The Bowing Process

*I*f you decide to make bowing a regular part of your practice, you will find that it is indeed simple. After a few times, you probably will not have to think about the individual bow at all; it will feel natural and normal to you.

But when you are first beginning, it might feel a bit awkward. This is simply because the motion is unfamiliar to you. In fact, you might even use some muscles that you don't use very often, and you might feel a little muscle soreness the next day. But don't worry—these discomforts will go away quickly, after only a few days of consistent practice.

In reality, the bow is easy on the body and is unlikely to cause physical harm, unless there is some preexisting injury or illness that impedes the bowing process.

As you read through the following steps, keep in mind that these steps are not actually separate. The entire bow should be done as one continuous, flowing motion, and there is no need to pause at any of the steps. One step leads seamlessly into the next, and one bow leads automatically into the next. This is part of its symbolic meaning, reminding us of the never-ending, cyclical flow of life. However, if in the beginning it is helpful to you to separate the steps, feel free to do so.

Breathing is also an important part of bowing. However, you won't see a great deal of instructions for breathing included here because breathing throughout the bow should remain natural. Over time, you will likely find that your breathing pattern synchronizes naturally with the bow itself, but this should not be rushed or forced. At first, simply be aware of your breathing without the need to control it. Soon, you will find that you naturally breathe in when you rise from the ground and breathe out as you lower to the floor.

Consider also the environment in which you perform bowing. It should be clean and free of distractions. If you like, you can play soft music to promote a sense of sacredness in the room. You might even try lighting a candle or some incense to help create a better mood. None of these things are necessary, but they might foster a greater sense of conviction and dedication in your mind.

There is no set time of day during which you should bow. Many people find that morning is a great time to bow, since it is a gentle way to get your body moving and your mind focused for the day. One practitioner (Kevin Twomey, Honolulu, HI) says, "When I do bowing in the morning, there is a marked difference for the rest of the day. I am able to focus on how to create the most with the day. The effects of bowing clear my mind of unnecessary clutter." Other people like to end their day with bowing as a way to release accumulated emotions and burdens. Another practitioner writes: "I've bowed at many different times of day. At the moment, I am bowing in the evening. When I bow in the evening, I clear out any stress or worries from the day and gain a new perspective on anything that's been on my mind" (Michela Mangiaracina, Sedona, AZ). Some people even bow in the morning and in the evening, to create a set of energetic bookends for their day.

Above all, remember that mind-set is far more important than form. While there is an ideal posture and movement, the attitude you bring to your bowing is the key to successful training. If you strive to approach bowing with a humble and sincere mind, you are bound to achieve great benefit, even if your form is less than ideal.

STEP 1 Warm-up

Before you begin bowing, please take some time to prepare yourself to bow. Otherwise, the tensions and frustrations from your day may follow you into your training session, rendering the experience less effective than it could be. The length of time you spend preparing to bow will vary, depending on the number of bows you plan to complete and how unfocused or tense you may feel in the moment. As a general rule of thumb, try to include at least five minutes of warm-up exercises before your daily bowing session.

Here you will find a collection of stretching, breathing, and relaxation exercises. You may do all of them if you like, or you can mix and match to suit your own particular needs. Feel free to use other exercises, so long as they help achieve a relaxed body and focused body and mind. For illustrated instruction of these exercises, please see the book *Dahn Yoga Basics* or the DVD *Dahn Yoga Essentials*.

❧ Full-Body Joint Opening ❧

This series of exercises can be used to open up the joints of the body that are used most in bowing. They are meant to flow easily from one to the next, so once you have familiarized yourself with them, they should not require much time. If you have any problems in particular joints, you might want to spend a little extra time warming up those areas.

Neck

1. Stand with your shoulders relaxed and your feet parted shoulder-width.
2. Drop your chin toward your chest and slowly begin to rotate your head to the right.
3. Roll your head back, feeling the stretch in the chin and neck.
4. Continue to rotate your head until you return to the original position.
5. Repeat this motion 5–10 times and then another 5–10 times in the opposite direction.

Shoulders

1. Keeping your arms relaxed, squeeze your shoulder blades together.
2. Bring your shoulders up toward your ears and then bring them forward, as if to touch them together in front of your chest.
3. Push your shoulders toward the ground and then down.
4. Continue the motion, making circular motions with your shoulders.
5. After 5–10 rotations, switch to the opposite direction.

Hip Joints

1. Rotate your hips in a large circle, pushing as far in all directions as possible. Keep your knees straight.
2. Repeat 5–10 times and then repeat in the opposite direction.

Knees

1. Bring your hands down to your knees with your palms resting lightly on your kneecaps.
2. Rotate your knees around to the right 5–10 times, and then switch direction.

Ankles

1. Place the toes of one foot on the ground with your heel up.
2. Place light pressure on your foot as you rotate on your toes and the ball of the foot.
3. After 5–10 rotations, switch directions.

❄ Full-Body Stretch ❄

This series of stretches will help warm up your muscles before you begin. Like the joint exercises, they are meant to flow together as one easy-to-follow sequence. To avoid muscle soreness, you might want to perform these exercises after bowing, as well as before.

Upward Reach

1. Stand with your shoulders relaxed and your feet slightly parted.
2. Clasp your hands together, your fingers interweaved together.
3. Lift your hands up and reach upward with your palms up. Inhale and push upward as much as you can, feeling the stretch through the upper body.
4. Exhale as you return to the original position. Repeat 3 times.

Side Bend

1. From the Upward Reach position, reach up once again, pushing your palms upward.
2. As you inhale, bend your body to the side, keeping your palms upward.
3. Exhale and return to the original position. Repeat 3 times.

Forward Bend

1. Keeping your hands interweaved as before, inhale and push your palms forward, keeping your palms facing outward.
2. Keeping your legs straight, bend forward at the waist, pushing forward with your hands until you feel a deep stretch in the lower back and legs. Inhale as you push forward. Keep your back straight and look at the back of your hands.
3. Exhale and return to the original position. Repeat 3–5 times.

Downward Reach

1. Again with your hands clasped together, reach your hands down toward the ground. Keep your legs straight as you push down with your palms. Look at the back of your hands.

2. Gently bounce your upper body 5–10 times to loosen the hamstrings on the back of the legs.
3. Exhale and return to the original position.

Downward Twist
1. Again with your hands clasped together as in the Downward Reach, reach your hands down toward the ground, but this time twist your body and reach over toward the outside of one foot. Keep your legs straight as you push down with your palms.
2. Gently bounce your upper body 5–10 times, feeling the light twist in the lower back.
3. Exhale and return to the original position, and then repeat on the opposite side.

❧ Brain Wave Vibration ❧
Ilchi Lee, the founder of Dahn Yoga and Brain Education, believes that this simple training method is the most effective brain training method. He contends that it encompasses all five steps of Brain Education and is a great way to prepare body, mind, and spirit for bowing.

1. Stand on a stable surface with your feet shoulder-width apart. Bend your knees so that your hips lower slightly. Allow your arms to drop forward slightly, and relax your shoulders completely.

2. Close your eyes and begin to bounce your hips up and down, following a rhythm that feels natural for your body.

3. Focus on exhaling and releasing tension from your body. Continue bouncing gently for five or more minutes until your body feels fully relaxed.

4. When you are fully relaxed, begin to follow your own vibration. There is no right or wrong posture at this point—just follow what feels natural to you. The vibration may be intense or gentle, depending on your particular needs. You may feel compelled to make dancelike movements as well.

5. As you return to full consciousness, shake out your arms and legs. Breathe in deeply, exhale fully, and sweep down your arms and torso with your palms.

❦ Chest Breathing ❦

If you have had an extremely stressful day, before bowing you might want to do a few minutes of chest breathing before you begin. It is a simple form of breath work, and it is effective for releasing stress quickly.

1. Lie down in a comfortable place that is not too hard or too soft.
2. Bring your arms to the side, 45 degrees from the body, with your palms facing the ceiling. Part your feet shoulder-width.
3. Focus on relaxing your body, releasing tension from each area, one by one.
4. Breathe in through your nose and out through your mouth slowly, but naturally.
5. Focus on the up-and-down movement of the chest.

STEP 2 Centering

Now that you have relaxed your body and mind, you are ready to begin the actual bow. In the first part, simply stand straight up with your palms together in the prayer position. During this time, you should close your eyes and focus on your lower abdomen (*dahn-jon*), which is the center of your energy system. By focusing here, you will further calm your energy and focus your mind on bowing.

1. Stand as straight as possible with feet together.
2. Place your palms together, about 2–3 inches from the chest. Keep your shoulders relaxed and breathe naturally.
3. Close your mind, and focus your mind and energy in the lower abdomen.
4. Imagine heaven energy entering the *beak-hoe* point on the top of the head and circulating throughout your body.

The simple act of standing symbolizes the human being's special relationship with heaven and Earth. Among Earth's creatures, humans are unique in their ability to stand fully upright. This reflects our special role as the bridge between heaven and Earth. Just as your feet remain solidly planted on the ground and your head is in the sky, the human being retains both earthly and heavenly attributes. It is the task of every person to find the proper, balanced expression of both these elements. In both East and West, palms placed together in front of the heart suggest reverence and sincerity.

STEP 3 Gathering Heaven

The third step of the bowing process involves gathering the energy of heaven into the heart. Do not worry about actually feeling this energy; it is really as much a symbolic act as anything. The important thing is to experience the sense of expansion and opening as you complete the movement.

1. From the centering posture, bring your hands down and toward the sides of your body.
2. Extending your arms outward, turn your palms upward and begin to lift your arms upward.
3. Bring your hands back together above your head in the prayer position.
4. Slowly bring your hands back down to the chest.

This part of the bow symbolizes the growth process that is always part of life. The act of extending your arms upward and outward can be likened to a flower blooming in springtime. For human beings, true growth means developing an awareness of one's divine nature and intrinsic connection to heaven. When we bow we symbolically gather heaven's energy into our heart so that we might live more compassionate, fulfilling lives.

STEP 4 Half-bow

The half-bow is used on its own in many cultures as a gesture of humility and respect. If you like, you may wish to add a half-bow to the beginning or ending or both of your bowing routine. The half-bow is the halfway point in the entire full-bow process, and it represents the transitions that are part of life: heaven to Earth, life to death, growth to decline, and so forth.

1. Keeping your hands together at your chest, slowly bend forward at the waist. Keep your legs straight.
2. Pause briefly once you have achieved an angle of approximately 90 degrees.

Now that we have filled ourselves with the energy of heaven, we must humble ourselves or risk the corruption that comes with spiritual pride. By bending forward, we offer the heavenly energy gathered through our *baek-hoe* to others, rather than simply taking it into ourselves, for it is through giving, rather than merely receiving, that we can exponentially accelerate our growth process.

STEP 5 Lowering to the Knees

In many cultures, bowing onto the knees represents a much deeper level of humility than bowing at the waist. In Western cultures, prayer is often done while kneeling because it suggests absolute humility and submission to God. It represents a true willingness to surpass ego and pride, which leads to greater blessing in the end.

1. From the half-bow position, raise the upper body slightly as you bend the knees.
2. Lower your knees all the way to the ground, being careful to maintain your balance. (Feel free to modify the kneeling process so that it is safe and comfortable for you.)

Just as a beautiful flower must eventually wither to the ground, all things that grow from the Earth must eventually return to the Earth. Life and death are all part of the grand cycle of existence. To resist these inevitabilities is both prideful and futile. The same is true for our individual process of growth and maturation. If we are to create ourselves anew, we must also be willing to cast off and destroy what does not serve our higher selves.

STEP 6 Forehead to the Earth

Now, from the kneeling position, you will lower yourself completely to the ground in a gesture of complete acceptance. This is a relaxed stance, helping you calm your mind and body together. Through it you can feel ultimate connection to Earth.

1. From the kneeling position, bring your palms to the ground so that you are on all fours.
2. Lower your upper body down so that your buttocks rest against your calves, your chest is against your knees, and your forearms are on the ground.
3. Carefully bring your forehead to the ground, feeling Earth energy entering your "third eye" (*in-dang*) point, the energy point on your forehead.

Regardless of how rich, talented, or intelligent you are, your life is completely and utterly dependent on the Earth and the bounties she provides. No form of life, from the smallest amoeba to the most complex organism, could exist without her. Through this gesture, you can visualize the miraculous process of growth from fetus to adult.

STEP 7 Heaven, Earth, and Human as One

Now that you have taken the position of complete humility and acceptance, you have prepared yourself to enter the stage of growth once again. Just as you began, you once again gather the energy of heaven through your palms to help fulfill the human role as intermediary between heaven and Earth. Imagine a lotus flower blooming on the crown of your head, indicating spiritual growth.

1. Keeping the previous position, slowly turn your palms upward.
2. With your head still on the ground, lift your hands up in a receiving gesture.

Just as the wilted flower decays and helps give rise to the new flower, the shedding of our old selves gives rise to the new. The spark of life, and gift from heaven, must be received with humility and grace. We turn our palms toward heaven in a gesture of reverent receptivity. With the spark of life received, we are ready to begin again as a new being.

STEP 8 **Return**

The final step marks the end of the bowing cycle, and like everything in life, this ending is also a beginning. It is in this ending that we also find the symbolic beginning of new life, represented by the act of returning to the upright position.

1. Bring your palms back to the floor and lift yourself up onto your hands and knees.
2. Curl your toes under and lift yourself back into the standing position, being careful to keep your balance.
3. Bring your hands together in front of your chest.

The completion of the bowing cycle represents the completion of the soul, the ultimate purpose of human life. Of course, completion is not achieved through a single cycle. Just as you practice a skill to perfect it, you must go through seemingly endless cycles of reinvention to find fulfillment and completion. Likewise, the completion of one bow leads to the next.

When you have completed the total number of bows you wish to complete in a session, spend a few minutes sitting quietly or do a few minutes of Brain Wave Vibration (see page 66). This will help extend the feeling of emptiness that comes with bowing.

As you begin to practice the art of bowing, realize that like everything else it does not have to be perfect. Feel free to adapt your bow as needed to make it more doable for you. Many people need to boost themselves up from the lowest position or find that their balance is a little off at first. If you have some sort of injury, especially to the knees or back, you should redesign your bow to suit your needs. If you have high blood pressure or suffer from vertigo, be careful raising and lowering yourself from the ground. As with any exercise, seek your doctor's opinion about its suitability for your physical condition.

If you are at all worried about your ability to complete the full bow safely, reduce the bowing process to a simple, sincere half-bow from the waist. If even that is hard, a simple, gracious lowering of the head is fine. Remember that a single adapted bow executed with compete sincerity is worth a million "perfect" bows done with a prideful mind or as a thoughtless habit. If you bow with people who are more athletic than you, don't worry. The ability to perform a bow well does not guarantee good results. Really, the results of bowing training can be truly assessed only by the one experiencing it, not by anyone observing it.

How you decide to incorporate bowing into your life is entirely up to you. You may decide to do many bows daily or just a few. Either way, if practiced with a positive, sincere attitude, you are likely to discover that bowing will become a natural part of your life. Its form reflects the constant ebb and flow of life, and through it you will likely gain great insight and inspiration, making your journey on the sea of life a calm and joyful ride.

APPENDIX I Quick Guide to Bowing

In chapter five you will find a detailed description of the bowing process. Here is a simplified overview of each step, in case you need a quick reminder.

STEP 1 WARM-UP
Relax your mind and body through stretching, breathing, and relaxation exercises.

STEP 2 CENTERING

Keeping your energy centered in your lower abdomen (*dahn-jon*), bring your hands to "prayer position" in front of your chest. Close your eyes and focus on receiving heavenly energy through the top of your head (*baek-hoe*).

STEP 3 GATHERING HEAVEN

Bring your hands down and to the outside with palms facing upward. Bring your palms back together over your head and draw your hands down the center line of your body, returning them to the prayer position in front of your chest.

Step 4 Half-bow at Waist
Bend forward at the waist, creating a 90-degree angle with your body.

Step 5 Lowering the Knees
Bend your knees and lower your upper body toward the ground.

Step 6 Forehead to the Earth
Bring your forehead (*in-dang*) to the floor. Keep your palms and the tops of your feet flat on the ground.

Step 7 Heaven, Earth, and Human as One
Turn your palms up and lift them toward heaven, focusing on the sensation in the center of your palms (*jang-shim*).

Step 8 Return
Lift your upper body and bring your hands back together. Curl your toes under your feet and lift your entire body back to the standing position.

Here are some simple guidelines to follow when bowing.

Dos

✓ Choose a reasonably quiet location with a flat surface to practice.

✓ Commit to a particular number of bows that you will complete daily—perhaps 21 or 103.

✓ Prepare your mind and body with Brain Wave Vibration and a few stretches before you begin.

✓ Modify your bow if you have knee problems or any other physical limitation.

✓ Wear loose-fitting clothing with sturdy material on the knees.

✓ If you like, find a bowing partner to help keep each other motivated.

✓ Use a cushion or yoga mat to protect your knees.

✓ Remove your shoes while bowing.

✓ Keep both sides of the body as symmetrical as possible during each bow.

✓ Breathe naturally and at a comfortable pace.

✓ Consult your physician about your physical readiness to bow, especially if you have any preexisting physical problems.

Don'ts

✗   Don't practice bowing if you are not willing to focus sincerely on it in the moment.

✗   Don't worry about having perfect form when you begin. Sincerity is more important.

✗   Avoid drinking large quantities of liquid immediately before or during bowing.

✗   Avoid eating large meals immediately before bowing.

✗   Don't force your breath.

✗   Stop bowing or modify your bow if you feel dizzy or off-balance.

✗   Don't bow so fast that you become short of breath.

APPENDIX 2 Bowing Q&A

What should I do if I feel bored during bowing?

This is normal, especially if you are doing long sets of bows or have been doing the same practice for a long time. The important thing is to not judge the feeling. If you focus on the feeling and decide it is "bad," you are only keeping yourself trapped in the thinking mind. Boredom is simply a habit of the thinking mind, which loves to be entertained with new information all the time. In a way, feeling bored means you are on the right track because your thinking mind is no longer getting the flow of information that it is addicted to. Instead of judging the feeling, just watch it and let it pass. ❧

My mind is always so busy during bowing. What do I do?

This is normal. Your mind is used to always being busy, and there is no reason for it to stop just because you are bowing. The best solution is to shift it toward the bow itself. If your mind is straying, concentrate on some aspect of the bowing movement, perhaps breathing, sensations in the body, or the motion of the arms and legs. Focusing on the lower body is especially helpful to bring the energy down from the head. You might also try using some positive mantra to focus the mind on something you would like to achieve or experience. For example, you could repeat to yourself, "I can do it" or "I am healthy and happy" or "I am one with all things." ❧

When should I bow?

You can bow during any time of day, but morning and evening are most popular among practitioners. In the morning, bowing can prepare your mind for the day, and in the evening, bowing can release burdensome thoughts and emotions before you go to bed. Some people even do both. Try different times and see what works for you. ❧

How many times should I bow?

There is no correct number of bows to do. You can do as many or as few as feels right to you. Often people choose numbers that are meaningful to them (see pages 54–55). You might want to start with a small number, such as 21. Many experienced practitioners seem to prefer doing 103, which can be completed in about fifteen to twenty minutes, as a daily practice. If you find that counting is distracting, you can just choose an amount of time to bow, such as fifteen minutes or a half hour.

Sometimes people do a small number of bows very slowly as a way to develop mindful awareness. Occasionally people do longer sets of bowing, as many as 1,000 or 3,000. This is usually done as an advanced training method to prepare the mind and body very deeply. You should attempt this only after preparing the mind and body carefully. ❧

My knees hurt when I bow. What should I do?

Knee trouble is a common complaint among first-time bowers. If you have serious problems with your knees, you should check with your doctor to make sure it is okay to bow. In the case of severe problems, you may need to eliminate the bending of the knees and do a simple half-bow from the waist. But for most people, it is just a matter of time before the pain subsides. Everyone should complete a few warm-up exercises before they bow, including some exercises to open up the knee joints (see page 63). Bowing is actually good for the knees because it is low impact and stretches the ligaments that surround the knee. After a few weeks of training, you should find that your knees are better than ever. ❧

How can I synchronize my breathing with my bowing?

There is only one way to perfect your breathing while bowing—practice. It is counterproductive to force your breath to match your movements. Some advanced practitioners can complete a full-bow cycle on one breath. This is almost never the case for beginners. Rather, simply breathe naturally and watch how your body moves in relation to your breath. Over time, they will become naturally synchronized. ❧

APPENDIX 3 Cultivating Sincerity

If you continue to practice bowing for a considerable length of time, you will inevitably lose your beginner's mind. When you start to bow, it is easy to remain sincere because it is all new to you and you naturally want to do your best. After a while, however, bowing may begin to seem like little more than a repetitive routine. It is at this point that you can fully examine your ability to practice with pure sincerity. In fact, bowing practice is often referred to as "sincerity training." When practiced diligently, it can become a great way to develop sincerity in all areas of your life.

The following passage contains wisdom about the art of sincerity from an ancient document known as the *Cham Jun Gye Kyung* or *The Book of the Righteous Life*. The full text contains 366 spiritual principles for those wishing to live a virtuous life. Fifty-four of these principles relate to sincerity, indicating the importance of sincerity to those seeking spiritual development. Six of these principles are translated and reproduced below.

The Cham Jun Gye Kyung is believed to have been handed down, generation after generation, from Korea's founding ancestor, the Dahn Gun, who presided over an enlightened society 5,000 years ago. It was first written in Chinese characters by the Eulpaso, prime minister of the Korea's Gorgureyo dynasty, more than 1,800 years ago. These ancient pearls of wisdom may help you maintain true sincerity in bowing and in your life.

❀ Spontaneous Sincerity ❀

Spontaneous sincerity is the sincerity that wells up naturally from within without reliance on anything else but oneself. If you take on a task without personal motives, but rather from a place of spontaneous sincerity, the task will get done naturally, without the need to strive for it. This will occur as naturally as summer follows spring and night follows day.

❀ Ceaseless Sincerity ❀

Ceaseless sincerity means keeping a sincere mind in every moment. There is a distinct difference between doing things continuously with utmost sincerity and just doing things without stopping. It is like the difference between genuine spiritual power and the kind of power that comes through greed and selfishness. In the beginning the difference might seem negligible, but over time it will grow as gigantic as the gap between the Earth and heaven.

❧ Endeavor ❧

Endeavoring means overcoming hardships and going forward without hesitation, even on occasions when you are tempted to quit or give in. When encountering a fork in the road, you must be able to choose the best path with conviction. When doing so, you may face many difficulties, but by overcoming them you will learn to do things on your own. When you make every possible effort, the roots of sincerity become deeper and strength comes naturally, without striving for it. As a result you will be able to carry out whatever tasks are at hand without worry or hesitation.

❧ No Desire ❧

When offering sincerity, you might have some desire attached to it at first. However, as your sincerity becomes deeper and deeper, the desire you had at the beginning decreases gradually and the sincerity increases.

When your sincerity reaches its fullest, the desire disappears completely and only the sincerity remains.

✻ Ceaseless Effort ✻

Just as little drops of water gather to make a mighty ocean, a new canyon can be carved into the earth as specks of dust are carried away by the wind day after day. The wind can create a canyon because it never gives up on its mission. Likewise, when you continuously offer sincerity, you can slowly but surely change the landscape of the world.

✻ Acting with the Power of Sincerity ✻

Acting with the power of sincerity means following one's unchanging will with sincerity and putting it into action. If you never stop listening to your inner convictions, the will becomes bigger and brighter, like the rising moon lighting up the dark sky. When you practice the power of sincerity, the strength gained at the beginning might seem small. However, if you keep doing it, you will eventually be able to gain strength capable of lifting thousands of tons of weight with one hand. But the results of your action will be unpredictable if your conviction is weak or the power of your sincerity fluctuates.

APPENDIX 4 Practice Record Chart

If you would like to make bowing a regular part of your meditation routine, it is probably best to start out by committing to a specific number of days. We suggest beginning with a twenty-one day session for a few reasons. First, twenty-one days is not an overwhelming number; just about anyone with any sort of schedule should be able to complete it without too much trouble. Second, twenty-one days is long enough to see real results from the practice. At the end of those twenty-one days, you can evaluate how you feel and decide if it is the right thing for you. Twenty-one days is thought to be the number of days required to make a new habit engraved in the brain. Thus, if you decide to continue bowing after the initial twenty-one days, it should be easy to keep going.

You can use the following chart to track your first twenty-one days. For each day that you practice, simply mark off the corresponding day. Before you begin, make sure that you are able to commit to all twenty-one days. Once you begin, there should be no missed days; otherwise, the effect will not be the same. You may also wish to supplement your twenty-one-day session by using BEST Life Media's *21-Day Journal*, which will allow you to reflect more deeply on your bowing experience.

Day 1

....

....

Day 2

....

....

Day 3

....

....

Day 4

....

....

Day 5

....

....

Day 6

....

....

Day 7

....

....

Day 8

Day 9

Day 10

Day 11

Day 12

Day 13

Day 14

Day 15

Day 16

Day 17

Day 18

Day 19

Day 20

Day 21

❧ Notes ❧

❧ Notes ❧

❧ Notes ❧

❀ Notes ❀

Works Cited

Aamodt, Sandra and Sam Wang. "Exercise and the Brain." *New York Times*, November 8, 2007.

Bresloff, Robert. "Exercise and the Lymphatic System." *Baby Boomer Magazine*, September 17, 2009.

Ernst, Carl, et al. "Antidepressant Effects of Exercise." *Journal of Psychiatry and Neuroscience* 31 (March 2006): 84–92.

Hartley, Howard. "An 'Exercise Snack' Plan." *Newsweek*, March 26, 2007, 60.

Sisson, Mark. "The Dangers of Muscle Imbalances and the Importance of Symmetry." www.wellsphere.com, October 21, 2009.

Wein, Harrison. "Stress and Disease." *NIH Word on Health*, October 2000.

Young, Scott. "Tips for Breaking Bad Habits and Developing Good Habits." www.pickthebrain.com, October 16, 2007.

Products of Related Interest

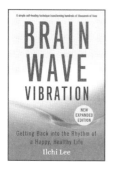

Brain Wave Vibration
Ilchi Lee

A powerful, easy-to-follow brain fitness and holistic healing method that helps people bring their bodies and minds back into balance for total health, happiness, and peace. The simplest form of practice merely requires moving your body to your own internal, natural healing rhythms in order to slow down and integrate your brain waves.

Paperback $14.95

Brain Wave Vibration: Audio Book with Guided Training Session
Ilchi Lee

This audio presentation of *Brain Wave Vibration* provides tips for practice and a complete, easy-to-follow training session, as well as profound insights into the nature of human happiness and fulfillment. Approximately 4 hours, 4 CDs

CD $24.95

Power of the Chun Bu Kyung
Ilchi Lee

This CD features various versions of the Chun Bu Kyung chanted by Ilchi Lee and Tao masters of the Sedona Mago Retreat Center. It is ideal for your morning and evening routine, and for centering, healing, and finding peace in meditation.

CD $19.95

Dahn Yoga Basics
Dahn Yoga Education
Learn the fundamentals of Dahn Yoga's highly effective mind-body training system. This easy-to-use reference text will help you perfect your postures as you learn the principles behind this gentle yoga. *Dahn Yoga Basics* is a must-have essential for all Dahn Yoga enthusiasts.
Paperback $18.00

Dahn Yoga Essentials: Featuring Brain Wave Vibration
Develop a strong and flexible body, boost your energy and vitality, and bring balance back into your life with this newest and most essential Dahn Yoga DVD. Let certified Dahn Yoga instructor Dawn Quaresima guide you through a one-hour training session that includes deep stretching exercises, meditative breathing techniques, Brain Wave Vibration, and an energy awareness meditation.
DVD $19.95

www.bestlifemedia.com
If you would like to learn more about our titles, please visit our website
www.bestlifemedia.com. Here you can browse through our books,
DVDs, and CDs to find exactly the right match
for your personal growth and fulfillment.

About the Author

Dahn Yoga Education is a collective of holistic health professionals dedicated to the creation of health, happiness, and peace on the individual and global levels. These contributors work together to develop educational materials based primarily on Dahn Yoga principles and practices. The publications and other products they create may be used in conjunction with Dahn Yoga practice or independently as a supplement to any self-development regimen.